D1538203

Texas

THE LONE STAR STATE

www.av2books.com

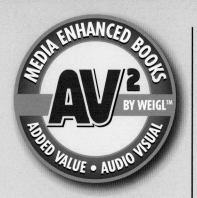

AV² provides enriched content that supplements and complements this boo
Weigl's AV² books strive to create inspired learning and engage young min
in a total learning experience.

Your AV² Media Enhanced books come alive with...

Audio
Listen to sections of
the book read aloud.

Key Words
Study vocabulary, and
complete a matching
word activity.

Video
Watch informative
video clips.

Quizzes
Test your knowledge.

Go to **www.av2books.com**,
and enter this book's
unique code.

Embedded Weblinks
Gain additional information
for research.

Slide Show
View images and
captions, and prepare
a presentation.

BOOK CODE

T 2 8 1 7 6

Try This!
Complete activities and
hands-on experiments.

... and much, much more

AV² by Weigl brings you media
enhanced books that support
active learning.

Published by AV² by Weigl
350 5th Avenue, 59th Floor
New York, NY 10118
Website: www.av2books.com   www.weigl.com

Library of Congress Cataloging-in-Publication Data

Parker, Janice.
 Texas / Janice Parker.
    p. cm. -- (A guide to American states)
 Includes index.
 ISBN 978-1-61690-816-4 (hardcover : alk. paper) -- ISBN 978-1-61690-492-0 (online)
 1. Texas--Juvenile literature. I. Title.
 F386.3.P353 2011
 976.4--dc23
                          2011019035

Printed in the United States of America in North Mankato, Minnesota

052011
WEP180511

Project Coordinator Jordan McGill
Art Director Terry Paulhus

Photo Credits
Every reasonable effort has been made to trace ownership and to obtain permission to reprint copyright material. The publishers would be pleased to have any errors or omissions brought to their attention so that they may be corrected in subsequent printings.

Weigl acknowledges Getty Images as its primary image supplier for this title.

Contents

AV² Book Code 2

Introduction 4

Where Is Texas? 6

Mapping Texas 8

The Land... 10

Climate 12

Natural Resources.................................. 14

Plants.. 16

Animals... 18

Tourism... 20

Industry 22

Goods and Services 24

American Indians 26

Explorers.. 28

Early Settlers.. 30

Notable People 32

Population 34

Politics and Government.......................... 36

Cultural Groups...................................... 38

Arts and Entertainment........................... 40

Sports 42

National Averages Comparison.............. 44

How to Improve My Community............ 45

Exercise Your Mind!............................... 46

Words to Know / Index........................... 47

Log on to www.av2books.com 48

Cowboys and ranching are a distinct part of Texas's culture.

Introduction

After Alaska, Texas is the largest state in area in the United States. For several years this state was a nation of its own. It was called the **Republic** of Texas. That all changed on December 29, 1845, when Texas became the 28th state to join the Union.

Texas is as large as Kentucky, Ohio, Indiana, and all of the Middle Atlantic and New England states put together. Its various regions include mountains, forests, deserts, plains, and a subtropical coast. Few other states have such a wealth of mineral resources as Texas. In the 20th century Texas became the leading producer and refiner of oil in the United States.

Parts of western Texas, such as the Guadalupe Mountains region, feature very dry areas.

A memorial to the famed Texas Rangers law-enforcement group is located in front of the State Capitol building in Austin.

The size and unique history of Texas have contributed to its culture. Ranchers, cattle herds, rodeos, and gushing oil wells all play an important part in Texas tradition. Although many people might imagine 10-gallon hats and cowboy boots when they think of Texas, there is much more than this to the state. For more than a century, Texas was part of Spain's North American empire, and for nearly 20 years it was part of Mexico. Hispanic food, culture, and architecture all help create a special atmosphere in the state.

Texas's nickname, the Lone Star State, comes from the state flag's one star on a blue strip. Beside it, a banner of white sits atop a banner of red. This flag was originally adopted in 1839 as the national flag of the Republic of Texas. After Texas joined the Union, it became the state flag. In the Texas flag, red stands for bravery, white stands for purity, and blue stands for loyalty.

Where Is Texas?

Texas sprawls across the south-central United States. The massive state spans 773 miles from its westernmost point to its easternmost locale, while 801 miles separate the northwest corner of the Texas panhandle and the southern tip of the state.

The Dallas/Fort Worth Airport ranks eighth in the world in the number of passengers served. The 30-square-mile facility is the fourth-largest airport in the world.

Motorists can travel around Texas on its nine primary interstate highways, as well as on many other federal and state highways. A number of these roads continue into Mexico. Texas also has two large international airports. Dallas/Fort Worth is located between the cities of Dallas and Fort Worth, and George Bush Intercontinental is in Houston. There are nonstop flights between Texas and Canada, Mexico, and countries in Asia, Europe, Central America, and South America.

The state's largest city, Houston, is located in the southeast, about 70 miles from the coast of the Gulf of Mexico. San Antonio, Texas's second most populous city, is 190 miles west of Houston. Austin, the state capital, is approximately 75 miles northeast of San Antonio. The huge Dallas-Fort Worth metropolitan area is about 170 miles north of Austin. Lubbock lies around 270 miles west of Forth Worth. Amarillo, in the Texas panhandle, is about 110 miles north of Lubbock. El Paso is in the far west on the Rio Grande. On the same river is Brownsville, the southernmost city in Texas.

I DIDN'T KNOW THAT!

Texas has a 367-mile coastline on the Gulf of Mexico.

In 1836 five sites served as temporary capitals of Texas. They were Washington-on-the-Brazos, Harrisburg, Galveston, Velasco, and Columbia. The capital was moved to Houston in 1837. In 1839 it was moved again to Austin, which became the state's permanent capital.

Texas has the right to split into five separate states under the terms of the 1845 resolution that welcomed the Republic of Texas into the United States.

The Houston skyline features 10 buildings that are at least 700 feet tall.

Mapping Texas

Texas shares its borders with four states, one country, and a major body of water. It is bordered by Louisiana and Arkansas to the east, Oklahoma to the north, and New Mexico to the west. The southeastern portion of Texas runs along the Gulf of Mexico, and the Rio Grande separates the state from the country of Mexico on the southwest.

Sites and Symbols

STATE SEAL
Texas

STATE BIRD
Mockingbird

STATE FLOWER
Bluebonnet

STATE FLAG
Texas

STATE MAMMAL (LARGE)
Texas Longhorn

STATE TREE
Pecan

Nickname The Lone Star State

Motto Friendship

Song "Texas, Our Texas," by William J. Marsh and Gladys Yoakum Wright

Entered the Union December 29, 1845, as the 28th state

Capital Austin

Population (2010 Census) 25,145,561 Ranked 2nd state

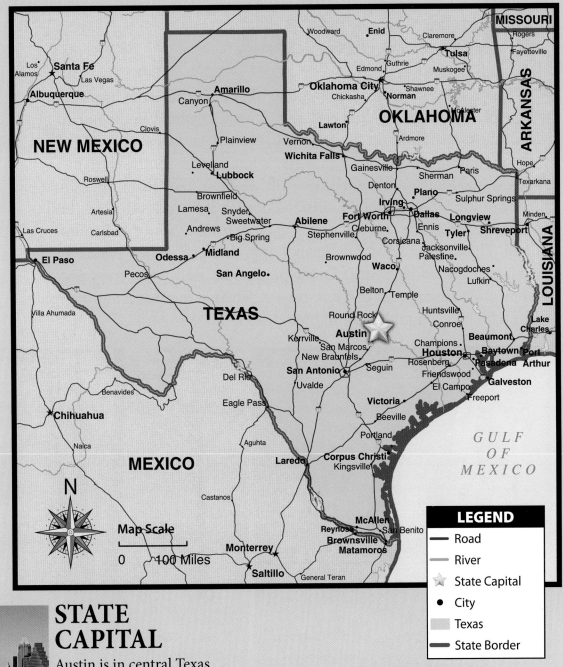

MISSOURI

Rogers
Claremore
Fayetteville
Tulsa
Muskogee
McAlester

OKLAHOMA

Woodward
Enid
Edmond
Guthrie
Oklahoma City
Shawnee
Chickasha
Norman
Lawton
Ardmore
Hope
Texarkana

ARKANSAS

LOUISIANA

Los Alamos
Santa Fe
Las Vegas
Albuquerque

NEW MEXICO

Canyon
Amarillo
Clovis
Plainview
Vernon
Wichita Falls
Gainesville
Sherman
Paris
Denton
Levelland
Lubbock
Plano
Brownfield
Irving
Dallas
Sulphur Springs
Lamesa
Snyder
Sweetwater
Fort Worth
Longview
Shreveport
Andrews
Abilene
Cleburne
Ennis
Tyler
Minden
Roswell
Artesia
Carlsbad
Stephenville
Corsicana
Jacksonville
Palestine
Nacogdoches
Las Cruces
Big Spring
Brownwood
Waco
Lufkin
El Paso
Odessa
Midland
Pecos
San Angelo
Belton
Temple
Huntsville
Villa Ahumada

TEXAS

Round Rock
Conroe
Lake Charles
Austin
Kerrville
Champions
Beaumont
Chihuahua
San Marcos
New Braunfels
Houston
Baytown
Pasadena
Port Arthur
San Antonio
Seguin
Rosenberg
Friendswood
Galveston
Naica
Del Rio
Uvalde
El Campo
Freeport
Benavides
Eagle Pass
Victoria
Beeville

GULF
OF
MEXICO

Aguhta
Portland

MEXICO

Castanos
Laredo
Corpus Christi
Kingsville
McAllen
Reynosa
San Benito
Monterrey
Brownsville
Matamoros
Saltillo
General Teran

N

Map Scale

0   100 Miles

LEGEND
— Road
— River
⭐ State Capital
● City
▢ Texas
— State Border

STATE CAPITAL

Austin is in central Texas on the north bank of the Colorado River. The community originally was called Waterloo. It was renamed in honor of Texas pioneer Stephen Austin in 1839, when it was chosen to be the capital of the recently formed Republic of Texas. Austin became the state capital when Texas joined the Union in 1845. It now is Texas's fourth-largest city, with a population of about 785,000.

Hawai'i   Alaska

United States

Texas

The Land

Texas has four major land regions. They are the Gulf Coastal Plain in the south and east, the Central Lowland in the north, the Great Plains in the far north, central, and western parts of the state, and the Basin and Range Region in the far southwest. The Gulf Coastal Plain covers about two-fifths of the state. Running from the lower Rio Grande to the Louisiana border, it includes the bays and barrier islands of the coast as well as plains running about 150 miles inland. The Central Lowland consists of prairie and rolling plains. In the Great Plains, which includes the panhandle, only a few trees and shrubs grow among seas of short grasses. The **barren** Basin and Range Region includes mountains and high desert.

EL CAPITAN

El Capitan in Guadalupe Mountains National Park is considered the most recognizable peak in the state. It is located near Texas's highest mountain, the 8,749-foot-tall Guadalupe Peak.

CADDO LAKE

Caddo Lake in northeastern Texas abounds with bald cypress trees and a variety of aquatic plants. It was the only natural lake in the state before it was dammed in the early 1900s.

PADRE ISLAND NATIONAL SEASHORE

This site, located near Corpus Christi in southern Texas, stretches 113 miles along the state's Gulf Coast. The protected area features white-sand beaches and dunes, grasslands, and marshes that serve as home to a variety of wildlife.

BIG BEND NATIONAL PARK

This park is located in a remote area of southwestern Texas along the Rio Grande. The unique desert region includes mountains, canyons, arid landscapes, and many types of plants and animals.

The Rio Grande is the largest river in the state. The waterway, which separates Texas and Mexico, winds along the border for about 1,250 miles after flowing through Colorado and New Mexico. Other large rivers in Texas include the Sabine, the Trinity, the Colorado, the Guadalupe, and the San Antonio.

Palo Duro Canyon, in the Texas panhandle, is the second-largest canyon in the United States. The gorge system is about 120 miles long and averages 6.2 miles in width. The canyon features many caves and chimney-shaped rock formations called hoodoos.

Texas averages 139 tornadoes per year, more than any other state.

Climate

T he climate of Texas varies in different parts of the state. Along the coast the weather stays mild throughout the year. The western highlands have dry, warm days and cold nights. Most of the rest of the state has warm, humid summers and cool winters. Texas often experiences weather extremes. Hurricanes can blow onshore from the Gulf of Mexico, and tornadoes touch down in north Texas every spring.

The warmest part of the state is the lower Rio Grande Valley. Average summer temperatures of 85° Fahrenheit and average winter temperatures of 60° F make it enjoyable year round. The coolest area is the windy panhandle, where summers average 79° F and winters average 35° F.

Average Annual Precipitation Across Texas

Yearly **precipitation** can vary greatly in Texas depending on location. What are some of the reasons why rainfall levels are so different around the state?

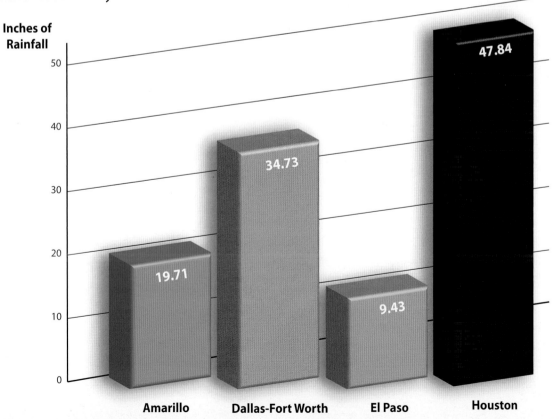

Inches of Rainfall

- Amarillo: 19.71
- Dallas-Fort Worth: 34.73
- El Paso: 9.43
- Houston: 47.84

Various drilling devices are used by Texas energy companies to extract oil from deep underground.

Natural Resources

Texas has many natural resources. Although less than one-tenth of Texas is forested, timber is an important **commercial** product. Some of the trees used for timber are pine, oak, elm, hickory, and magnolia. The good soil and rainfall in eastern Texas make for excellent farmland.

The state is especially rich in mineral resources. Texas has more petroleum reserves than any other state. Natural gas and coal are found in large quantities. Texas also has large reserves of helium, salt, sulfur, clay, and talc.

The Texas coast has a number of major **ports** for shipping and trade. The busiest port in the state in terms of the amount of cargo handled is the Port of Houston. Shrimp are the most important commercial catch in the Gulf of Mexico.

The Port of Houston is the second-busiest port in the United States. It handles almost 200,000 tons of cargo each year.

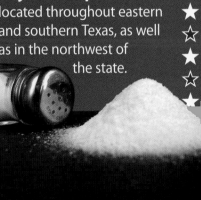

Plants

Texas is rich with fascinating plant life. The woodland areas of the state are home to pine and oak trees. Drier areas have mesquite, cactus, and sagebrush. The plains regions have hundreds of different types of grasses.

Thousands of plant species are native to Texas. Some 5,000 species of wildflowers bloom in the state. Bluebonnets, daisies, sunflowers, and asters are some of the most common flowers. The state plant of Texas is the prickly pear cactus. The fruit of the prickly pear is called *tunas*, and it makes delicious jelly. The flat pads, called *nopales*, are peeled and eaten as well. Grapefruits and many other citrus fruits are grown in Texas, although the plants are not native to the state.

PRICKLY PEAR CACTUS

The prickly pear is an edible variety of cactus most commonly found in the arid south and central Texas regions. Before the plant's fleshy pads can be eaten, its needles and hairlike spines must be removed. The prickly pear became the state plant in 1996.

BLUEBONNETS

The bluebonnet is a type of wildflower commonly seen growing along highways and rural roads in central and southern Texas. It blooms during the early spring. The bluebonnet was officially chosen as the state flower in 1971.

MESQUITE TREE

The mesquite tree is one of the most widely found trees in Texas. It can grow to a height of 30 feet but often is much smaller. When burned, mesquite wood adds a pleasant flavor to foods and is popularly used in Texas-style barbecue.

AGAVE

The agave is a type of spiky plant found in the southern and western United States. There are many species of agave. A sweetener called agave nectar can be extracted from the plant. Agaves also are used to make the alcoholic beverage tequila.

The Texas red grapefruit became the official state fruit in 1993. Texas's first grapefruit grove was planted in 1893, and the fruit soon became an important cash crop. The inside of grapefruits can be shades of yellow and red, but only red varieties have been produced in Texas since the 1960s.

Pecan trees usually grow to be 70 to 100 feet tall, but some have reached heights of more than 150 feet. The trees are the source of the popular nuts of the same name. Texas is one of the largest producers of pecans in the United States. The pecan tree was adopted as Texas's state tree in 1919.

Animals

Animal life abounds in Texas. The state has the most deer of any state in the nation. Jackrabbits, foxes, raccoons, pronghorns, and armadillos are other common Texas mammals. More than 100 species of snakes, including several poisonous types, live in Texas. The state also has many types of birds, including mockingbirds, hummingbirds, roadrunners, and prairie chickens.

Texas has several large bat colonies. At least 20 million bats live in Bracken Cave, near San Antonio, and 1.5 million fly nightly from beneath the Congress Street Bridge in Austin.

Whooping cranes spend their winters in the Aransas National Wildlife Refuge. In the 1940s there were fewer than 20 whooping cranes left in the world. **Conservation** workers bred the birds and released them into the wild. Now there are more than 200 cranes living outside of captivity.

ARMADILLOS

The armadillo is covered in plates of tough skin that serve as armor. The cat-sized mammal also has sharp claws that help it burrow into the ground. The armadillo was adopted as Texas's official state small mammal in 1995.

PRONGHORNS

The pronghorn, found across western Texas, is the only horned animal that sheds its horns every year. It also is the fastest North American mammal. It can reach speeds of about 60 miles an hour.

BLACK-TAILED JACKRABBITS

Black-tailed jackrabbits are common throughout most of Texas, particularly in the state's grassy plains and arid scrublands. Also called desert hares, they have long hind legs and huge ears that let off excess heat.

ROADRUNNERS

Roadrunners are found throughout the woodlands, grasslands, and deserts of Texas. They are long-legged birds that can run at a speed of more than 15 miles per hour. Although roadrunners are able to fly, they spend most of their time on the ground.

Whooping cranes are the tallest North American birds. They stand 5 feet tall and can have a wingspan as wide as 7.5 feet.

The Western diamondback rattlesnake is the most widespread poisonous snake found in Texas. It can grow to be more than 7 feet long, but usually it is between 3 and 4 feet. When rattlesnakes feel threatened, they coil their bodies and shake the rattle-like structure at the tip of their tail as a warning.

Tourism

About 190 million U.S. travelers made trips to Texas destinations in 2009. The tourism sector of the state's economy earned more than $50 billion that year.

Tourist attractions are located all over the state. Many people come to visit natural areas such as Big Bend National Park and Guadalupe Mountains National Park. The Gulf Coast has many beaches and **resorts**.

San Antonio is the state's top tourist destination. There visitors flock to the Alamo, site of a bloody battle during Texas's fight for independence from Mexico. Another major attraction is the city's River Walk, a tree-lined path with restaurants, shops, and boat docks along the San Antonio River. Every spring thousands of music fans gather in Austin for the South by Southwest music festival. Six Flags Over Texas, near Dallas, is a popular amusement park with a historical theme.

THE ALAMO

The Alamo, Texas's most popular tourist stop, was originally the chapel of a mission. Later it was used as a fort during Texas's war of independence. Each year more than 2 million people visit the site where Jim Bowie, Davy Crockett, and many other heroic men died battling the Mexican army.

SPACE CENTER HOUSTON

This facility is the visitor center of NASA's Lyndon B. Johnson Space Center, the complex where human spaceflight training and monitoring take place. The attraction offers astronaut-related exhibits, theaters, and tours of the grounds.

GUADALUPE MOUNTAINS NATIONAL PARK

Guadalupe Mountains National Park, located in west Texas, has four of the highest peaks in the state and more than 80 miles of hiking and walking trails. In addition to the rocky peaks, the park features desert landscapes and canyons.

GALVESTON ISLAND

Galveston Island in south Texas is a Gulf Coast resort that offers 32 miles of beaches. Visitors there can also enjoy a variety of restaurants, art galleries, and antique shops.

I DIDN'T KNOW THAT!

Six Flags Over Texas, in Arlington, is the most-visited amusement park in the state. The facility, which opened in 1961, features about 45 rides.

The Lady Bird Johnson Wildflower Center in Austin was created in 1982 for plant research and to educate people about the importance of native plants.

SeaWorld San Antonio is a very popular marine-life theme park that features dolphins, killer whales, and sea lion shows. The attraction also offers various exhibits, a water park, and rides such as roller coasters and a water flume.

Industry

S ince the first Texas oil boom in 1901, the oil and natural gas industry has played an important role in the state's economy. The mining, processing, and shipping of oil and natural gas are valuable sources of income in Texas. These products are sent through pipelines, in tanker trucks, and on ships to the rest of the country and the world.

Industries in Texas
Value of Goods and Services in Millions of Dollars

The mining industry is a very significant part of the Texas economy. Can you name some of the important minerals that are mined in the state?

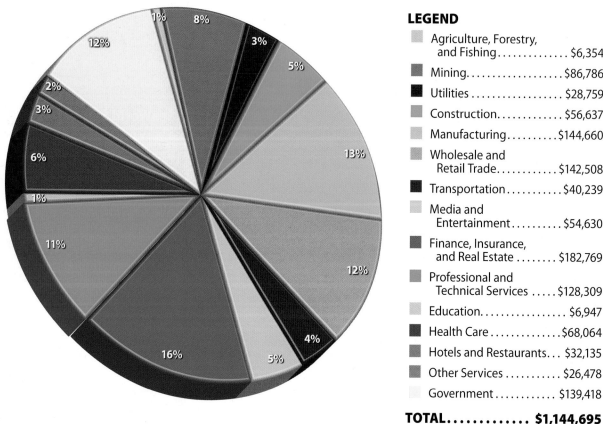

LEGEND

Agriculture, Forestry, and Fishing	$6,354
Mining	$86,786
Utilities	$28,759
Construction	$56,637
Manufacturing	$144,660
Wholesale and Retail Trade	$142,508
Transportation	$40,239
Media and Entertainment	$54,630
Finance, Insurance, and Real Estate	$182,769
Professional and Technical Services	$128,309
Education	$6,947
Health Care	$68,064
Hotels and Restaurants	$32,135
Other Services	$26,478
Government	$139,418
TOTAL	**$1,144,695**

Percentages do not add to 100 because of rounding.

Factories in Texas manufacture foods such as baked goods, soft drinks, and meat products. Technology companies build computers and other electronic equipment. Textiles, cars and trucks, and heavy equipment are also manufactured in the state. About one out of every six non-farm workers in Texas has a job in mining, logging, manufacturing, or construction.

Texas is among the top agricultural states, with more than three-fourths of its land used for farming or grazing. In dry areas, **irrigation** helps farmers grow crops such as cotton and grain.

The Spindletop oil gusher near Beaumont on January 10, 1901, marked the beginning of the modern petroleum industry in Texas.

Midlothian, located south of Dallas and Fort Worth, is known as the Steel and Cement Capital of Texas.

Texas produces more cattle than any other state.

More people work in the mining, oil, and gas industry in Texas than in any other state.

Texas produces and refines the most crude oil in the country. More than 400 million barrels of crude oil were produced in Texas in 2009.

Texas leads all states in the production of cotton and cottonseed.

Goods and Services

The Texas economy is among the largest in the country. Agriculture has always been important to the state. Meat from livestock, grain, dairy products, apples, and pecans are just a few of Texas's agricultural products. With more than 245,000 farms and ranches, Texas has more farmland and pasture than any other state.

Besides pigs and cattle bred for meat, Texas farmers also raise sheep and goats for wool. The state is famous for its Angora goats, which produce the soft wool known as mohair. Texas also produces many of the vegetables and fruits eaten in the country, including watermelons and honeydews. The state fruit, the red grapefruit, is grown in the lower Rio Grande area. Cotton and sorghum, which were once grown only in humid eastern Texas, are now major crops in the irrigated areas of the western plains. Rice, corn, and wheat are among the grains grown in the state.

With a herd of 200,000 Angora goats, Texas is responsible for about 90 percent of the mohair wool produced in the United States.

The oil industry accounted for much of Texas's economy for many years. The importance of oil is still strong, but it has decreased with the introduction of other industries. These industries include food processing and aircraft manufacturing. Machinery and equipment production also bring a great deal of money into Texas.

Electronics are moneymakers as well. Texas Instruments is a major producer of electronic goods and military communications systems. Dell Computers, Apple Computers, and IBM also have large facilities in the state.

Chemicals, including petroleum products, are the leading manufactured goods in Texas. Important products include benzene, fertilizers, and sulfuric acid.

Almost one-fourth of the people who work drilling oil and gas wells in the United States are employed in Harris County, Texas.

American Indians

American Indians lived in Texas 10,000 to 12,000 years ago, and perhaps much earlier. These early people gathered fruits and nuts and used stone tools to hunt and butcher large game, such as bison, which are often called buffalo. Later groups lived in settled villages, made pottery and tools, and built large ceremonial mounds.

By the beginning of the 1500s dozens of American Indian groups lived in the Texas area. Two of the largest groups were the Caddo and the Jumano. The Caddo lived in farming villages near the Red River in northern and eastern Texas. They grew corn and vegetables and made homes out of grass and wood poles. The Jumano lived along the Rio Grande in the southwest. They farmed and traded with hunters from farther north. The Karankawa were **nomads** who roamed the Gulf Coast. They ate fish, small game, plants, and insects.

Apache Indians were known for being fierce warriors and expert hunters.

The Apache and the Comanche arrived later from the north, roaming the plains on horseback and hunting bison. They ate the meat and used the rest of the animal to make shelters, blankets, clothing, and tools. These peoples also raided the settled farming villages of the region and often battled each other. By the 1700s the Apache and Comanche were feared by American Indians and Europeans alike.

During the 1800s, Comanche Indians fought many battles with Texas settlers who began to populate the tribe's hunting grounds.

I DIDN'T KNOW THAT!

The Caddo called themselves thecas, which meant "friends" or **"allies,"** because they banded together against Apache raiders. The Spanish spelled the word *tejas* or *texas* and used it to name the area where these people lived.

The Jornada Mogollon lived in western Texas until about 700 years ago. They decorated pottery and painted or chiseled many images on rocks in the region.

People known as the Basket Makers, ancestors of today's Pueblo Indians, lived along the Pecos River. They wove baskets and sandals from the leaves of plants.

The Atakapa, the Tonkawa, and the Akokisa were other tribal groups who lived near the Gulf Coast.

In the 1500s about 300,000 American Indians lived in what is now Texas. Today there are around 200,000 people of American Indian descent in the state.

Explorer Álvar Núñez Cabeza de Vaca's historic journey through Texas and the American Southwest began as a royal Spanish expedition that sought to colonize North America. About 600 men set sail from Spain, but Cabeza de Vaca was among only four men known to have survived the adventure.

Explorers

The first explorers in Texas were Spaniards. In 1519, Alonso Álvarez de Pineda mapped out the Gulf of Mexico coast and likely went inland to what is now Texas. In 1528, Álvar Núñez Cabeza de Vaca's ship was wrecked near what is now Galveston. For years afterward, he and three other survivors wandered through the Texas region and the American Southwest. In 1536 they reached a Spanish settlement in Mexico. There they told tales of cities full of gold and jewels that they had heard from the region's natives.

In 1540 the explorer Francisco Vázquez de Coronado traveled from Mexico into the American Southwest. He and his army found no sign of riches. In 1598, Juan de Oñate started exploring the area above the Rio Grande looking for silver mines and hoping to spread Christianity. He began the establishment of missions and ranches along the upper Rio Grande. At this time Spain had little interest in the rest of Texas.

French explorer René-Robert Cavelier, sieur de La Salle, created a colony in southeast Texas in 1685. He claimed the area for France and hoped to use it to fight the Spanish presence in Mexico. Within a few years, though, all French settlers at La Salle's colony had died from disease or been killed. The Spanish decided to take over the land. Over the next century they built missions throughout Texas. Many had military outposts nearby to protect inhabitants from hostile tribes.

Timeline of Settlement

European Exploration

1519 Spanish explorer Alonso Álvarez de Pineda maps the Texas coastline.

1528 Álvar Núñez Cabeza de Vaca and crew begin exploration of Texas after being shipwrecked near Galveston.

1541 Francisco Vázquez de Coronado explores part of the Texas panhandle.

1598 Juan de Oñate claims all land surrounding the Rio Grande in the name of Spain's King Philip II.

Early Colonization

1685 French explorer René-Robert Cavelier, sieur de La Salle, establishes the Fort St. Louis colony and claims the Texas region for France.

1687 La Salle is killed by his own men. Soon after, the remaining French colonists die or are killed by Indians.

1700s Spain establishes Catholic missions throughout the Texas region.

Independence From Spain, Then Mexico

1821 Mexico, including what is now Texas, gains independence from Spain.

1823 The Mexican government grants Stephen Austin a contract to bring 300 families from the United States into Texas, thereby establishing the first major colony.

1835 Texas colonists begin an armed revolt against Mexico.

1836 After a series of clashes, including the Alamo battle, the Republic of Texas is established.

Statehood and Civil War

1845 Texas is admitted to the Union as the 28th state.

1861–1865 Texas secedes from, or leaves, the Union and joins the Confederate States of America in 1861. The Civil War rages until 1865, when the Confederacy is defeated by the Union.

1870 Texas is readmitted to the Union as a state.

Early Settlers

I n 1820 the Spanish gave an American named Moses Austin permission to start an Anglo-American colony in Texas. However, he died in 1821 before he had the chance to recruit colonists for the planned settlement. In 1823, soon after Mexico won independence from Spain, Austin's son Stephen was given approval to bring about 300 families to the area.

Map of Settlements and Resources in Early Texas

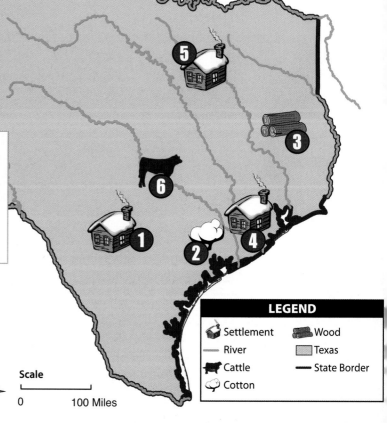

5 In 1841, Dallas is founded as a trading post. The settlement's location on the Trinity River and the fertile land surrounding the site attract farmers interested in growing cotton and other crops.

1 San Antonio is founded in 1718 as the Mission San Antonio de Valero. By 1803, the Mexican military occupies the mission, and its name is changed to the Mission del Alamo del Parras.

6 Cattle ranching is introduced to the Texas region by Spanish colonists before 1700. The Texas cattle industry's first big boom takes place from 1866 to the early 1880s.

2 In 1824, Stephen Austin founds the unofficial capital of his Texas colony at San Felipe de Austin, about 45 miles west of present-day Houston. Because of good soil and climate, cotton plantations are soon established nearby.

3 The lumber industry in Texas dates back to before the Texas Revolution of 1835-1836. During the mid-1800s, sawmills exist in several Gulf Coast settlements, as well as a number of inland locations. After the Civil War, the pine forests of east Texas become a major source of lumber.

4 In 1836, New York land developers John Kirby Allen and Augustus Chapman Allen found the city of Houston.

N

Scale

0   100 Miles

LEGEND

Settlement		Wood	
River		Texas	
Cattle		State Border	
Cotton			

The settlers moved to an area between the Colorado and Brazos rivers and called their colony San Felipe de Austin. The first few years were difficult. Crops failed, and the Karankawa people killed many settlers.

Over the next 15 years, 20,000 more Anglo-American settlers arrived, bringing 4,000 black slaves with them. Unhappy with the Mexican government, these settlers began fighting for independence in 1835. Much blood was shed in the war that followed. It was during this period that Texan forces were defeated at the famous battle of the Alamo. After the Texans won the Battle of San Jacinto on April 21, 1836, however, they succeeded in establishing the independent Republic of Texas. For the next nine years Texas remained independent. It joined the United States on December 29, 1845.

The Battle of the Alamo, the most famous conflict in Texas's fight for independence, took place from February 23 to March 6, 1836. Nearly all the Texan defenders were killed in the clash, and hundreds of Mexican troops also lost their lives.

I DIDN'T KNOW THAT!

Corpus Christi de la Isleta, established near El Paso in 1682, was the first Spanish mission within the modern boundaries of Texas.

Mission San José y San Miguel de Aguayo in San Antonio was established in 1720. San José became known as the Queen of the Missions because it was the largest mission in the area.

Spanish settlement in Texas was very thin. By 1800 there were only about 3,000 settlers of Spanish descent and 1,000 soldiers in Texas.

Mexico had laws against slavery. Many of the early settlers in Texas broke these laws by bringing their slaves to the area.

Many Americans from the Southern states moved to Texas during the first half of the 1800s. They often left signs saying "GTT," for "Gone to Texas," when they set out on their journeys.

Notable People

The citizens of Texas have a reputation for their pioneering spirit, determination, bravery, and ingenuity. These qualities certainly are evident in some of the famous people who were born or lived in the state. From colonial leaders and politicians to military heroes and business people, Texans have left their mark on U.S. history.

SAM HOUSTON (1793-1863)

Houston was born in Virginia and grew up in Tennessee. He became a Tennessee congressman and governor during the 1820s, then moved to Texas in the 1830s. He led rebel Texan forces to victory against the Mexican government, and he became the Republic of Texas's first president. After Texas entered the Union in 1845, Houston served as a U.S. senator from 1845 to 1859. He was elected governor of Texas in 1859 but resigned in protest two years later when the state joined the Confederacy. The city of Houston is named for him.

STEPHEN AUSTIN (1793-1836)

Born in Virginia and raised in Missouri, Austin came to Texas in the 1820s seeking to complete his late father's plan to establish an Anglo-American colony in what was then a Mexican province. After receiving permission from the Mexican government, Austin began moving hundreds of families into the region. He then helped establish laws for the colony and negotiated for the rights of the settlers. When Texas became an independent republic in 1836, Austin served as its first secretary of state. Thanks to his contributions, Austin is known as the Father of Texas.

LYNDON B. JOHNSON (1908-1973)

Johnson was the 36th president of the United States. Born near Stonewall, he eventually served as a Texas congressman and senator. In 1960, Johnson was elected U.S. vice president. He became president after John F. Kennedy's assassination in 1963. During his presidency, the country underwent many social reforms, but also was drawn deeper into the Vietnam War.

BARBARA JORDAN (1936-1996)

Born and raised in Houston, Jordan grew up to become the first African American woman from a Southern state to be elected to the U.S. House of Representatives. Prior to her time in Congress, in the 1970s, she became the first African American woman to serve as a Texas state senator.

GEORGE W. BUSH (1946-)

Bush, who was raised in Midland, served as Texas's governor before being elected the 43rd president of the United States in 2000. After the September 11, 2001, attacks, Bush led the country in a war against terrorism that included invasions of Iraq and Afghanistan. He is the son of the 41st U.S. president, George H. W. Bush.

I DIDN'T KNOW THAT!

Chester Nimitz (1885-1966), who was born in Fredericksburg, was a decorated admiral in the United States Navy. During World War II, he led Allied forces in the Pacific. His military achievements earned him Distinguished Service Medals from both the army and the navy.

Mary Kay Ash (1918-2001) was one of the most successful female business leaders in U.S. history. A native of Hot Wells, she went on to found Mary Kay Cosmetics in 1963. The company has become the largest direct seller of skincare products in the country.

Population

T exas has a highly diverse population. Many Texans are descended from people who came to the area from Mexico or from other parts of the United States. According to 2009 estimates, more than 46 percent of the population is of non-Hispanic European **ancestry**. Hispanic Americans make up about 37 percent of the population, and about 12 percent of Texans are African American. About 3.6 percent of the population is Asian American.

About 88 percent of Texans live in cities, suburbs, or towns. Counting the suburbs and smaller towns surrounding the central cities, Dallas–Fort Worth is the largest metropolitan area in the state, with more than 6.4 million people. Houston has about 5.9 million in its metropolitan area. The state also has hundreds of tiny towns.

Texas Population 1950–2010

Since 1950, Texas's population has increased during each 10-year period. Which decade saw the most population growth in the state? What are some reasons why Texas's population might have grown so much during that time?

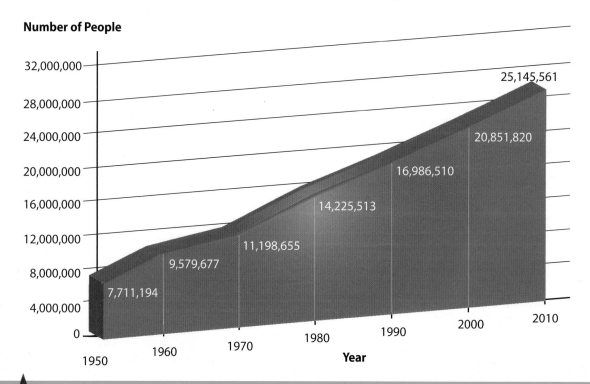

Number of People

Year	Population
1950	7,711,194
1960	9,579,677
1970	11,198,655
1980	14,225,513
1990	16,986,510
2000	20,851,820
2010	25,145,561

Thousands of Texas residents and tourists spend time eating and shopping at the River Walk in San Antonio, the state's second most populous city.

Most of Texas's population lives in the eastern part of the state.

The Dallas-Fort Worth metropolitan area's population alone is greater than that of 35 states.

Dallas has a population of 1,300,000. The only cities in Texas with more people are Houston with 2,258,000, and San Antonio with 1,374,000.

Houston is Texas's largest city, and the fourth most-populous city in the United States. About 27 percent of its residents are under the age of 18.

Politics and Government

Texas is governed under a constitution adopted in 1876. The government is divided into three sections. They are the legislative, executive, and judicial branches. The legislative branch includes the Senate and the House of Representatives, which make laws for Texas. There are 31 senators elected to four-year terms and 150 representatives elected to two-year terms. They decide on issues including how to spend state money.

The Texas State Capitol, located in Austin, was built between 1882 and 1888.

The governor is head of the executive branch and is elected for a four-year term. The governor makes sure that laws are carried out. The judicial branch is made up of the courts. Most judges in Texas are elected for four-year terms. Texas has a very complex system of local, district, and state courts. The state's highest courts are the Supreme Court and the Court of Criminal Appeals.

Texas is divided into 254 counties. There are more than 1,000 cities and towns, each with its own local government. In the U.S. Congress, Texas has two seats in the Senate. Because of its population growth, Texas will have 36 seats in the U.S. House of Representatives beginning in 2013. The state currently has 32 representatives in the U.S. House.

George W. Bush and his father, George H. W. Bush, are former U.S. presidents who made important contributions to Texas. Both men were successful oil businessmen in the state. The elder Bush also served as a Texas congressman, and his son was governor of the state from 1995 to 2000.

Texas's state song is called "Texas, Our Texas."

Here is an excerpt from the song:

Texas, our Texas! All hail the mighty State!
Texas, our Texas! So wonderful so great!
Boldest and grandest, Withstanding ev'ry test,
O Empire wide and glorious, You stand supremely blest.

[Refrain] God bless you Texas! And keep you brave and strong,
That you may grow in power and worth, Thro'out the ages long.

Texas, O Texas! Your freeborn single star,
Sends out its radiance to nations near and far.
Emblem of freedom! It sets our hearts aglow,
With thoughts of San Jacinto and glorious Alamo.

Cultural Groups

Hispanic culture has a long history in Texas. Many Hispanic Americans in the state are descended from people who lived in the area long before it became part of the United States. Others have come more recently from Mexico or other Latin American countries. Several Mexican holidays are celebrated in Texas. Parades and festivals on Cinco de Mayo, or May 5th in English, celebrate an 1862 Mexican military victory. September 16th marks the anniversary of Mexico's independence from Spain. Día de los Muertos, or Day of the Dead, is celebrated on November 1st and 2nd. It is a traditional Mexican holiday in which people remember their dead ancestors.

Hispanic music and food are very popular in Texas. Tex-Mex **cuisine**, a blend of foods traditionally eaten by the Indian and Hispanic people of south and west Texas, is now enjoyed around the country.

Each May 5th, the Mexican holiday of Cinco de Mayo is celebrated throughout Texas with music, dancing, and parades.

Cowboys have become central to Texas's cultural tradition. In the 1800s cattle abounded on the open Texas range. Cowboys would round up the animals and drive them hundreds of miles to market or to railroads where they could be shipped east. Though the great cattle drives lasted for only a few years, this period left a lasting impression on Texas dress and culture.

Cowboy clothing originated on cattle ranches in northern Mexico. It was originally designed to make cattle work easier. Cowboy jeans lack **rivets** on the back pockets, which could damage saddles. Leather chaps protect legs from rain and brush. Wide hats protect the head from sun, rain, and blowing dust. Pointy boots slip smoothly into stirrups. Chuck-wagon foods, such as barbecued steak and beans, are an important part of Texas cooking. Rodeos help keep the skills of cowboy culture alive.

Texas hosts many rodeos each year. Local cowboys often take part in these events.

Arts and Entertainment

Texas boasts several fascinating libraries and museums. The Texas State Library in Austin, established in 1839, is the state's oldest library. The Witte Museum in San Antonio has exhibits on the state's natural history, archaeology, and American Indian art and culture. There are also paintings and artifacts from the days of early settlers. San Antonio is also home to the San Antonio Museum of Art, which houses Greek and Roman antiquities, Asian art, and American paintings, as well as American Indian, Mexican, and Spanish colonial art.

Texas has a rich musical heritage. Blues music developed from African American work songs and religious music after the Civil War. Country and western music is popular in Texas. Fiddle and guitar are often played in traditional country and western songs. The state also has produced many popular rock, R&B, and pop artists.

Houston native Beyoncé Knowles was lead singer of the R&B group Destiny's Child before launching a very successful solo career. She also has acted in such hit movies as Dreamgirls.

Another type of music in Texas is a blend of Mexican and German influences. This music is called conjunto, which is Spanish for "together," or Tex-Mex music. People from southeast Texas tap their toes to zydeco music, which originated with the Creoles of neighboring Louisiana.

Many famous authors have come from Texas. Katherine Anne Porter, born in the tiny town of Indian Creek, was a leading novelist and short-story writer. Her collected stories won the **Pulitzer Prize** in 1965. Larry McMurtry wrote dozens of books and screenplays before he won the Pulitzer for his novel *Lonesome Dove* in 1986.

Every October the nation's largest state fair is held in Dallas. Country, blues, and rock musicians perform at the event, which also boasts the 212-foot Texas Star, the tallest Ferris wheel in the United States.

ZZ Top is a Houston-based rock trio that sometimes is called "That Little Ol' Band from Texas." The group was inducted into the Rock and Roll Hall of Fame in 2004.

I DIDN'T KNOW THAT!

Texans Tommy Lee Jones, Sissy Spacek, Jamie Foxx, and Renée Zellweger are successful actors who have all won Academy Awards.

Country music legends Willie Nelson, George Jones, and Waylon Jennings were all born and raised in Texas.

Buddy Holly, Roy Orbison, and Janis Joplin are three of the best-known rock musicians who have come from Texas.

Because of its dozens of music clubs and auditoriums, Austin calls itself "the live music capital of the world."

Selena Gomez, Jessica Simpson, and Hillary Duff are Texan entertainers who have been successful as both actresses and pop singers.

Sports

Texas has many professional sports teams. In Major League Baseball, the Houston Astros play in the National League and the Texas Rangers in the American League. The Rangers play their home games in Arlington, outside Dallas. The Dallas Cowboys have won the National Football League championship five times. The Houston Texans brought professional football back to Houston in 2002 after the Oilers left the city in 1996.

The state is home to three teams in the National Basketball Association, or NBA. They are the Dallas Mavericks, the Houston Rockets, and the San Antonio Spurs. Texas also claims the San Antonio Silver Stars, a team in the Women's National Basketball Association, or WNBA.

One major professional hockey team calls Texas home. The Dallas Stars play in the National Hockey League. The team moved from Minnesota to Texas in 1993 and won the Stanley Cup in 1999.

The Dallas Cowboys have long been a successful and popular National Football League franchise. The team has appeared in eight Super Bowls, and has won five of them.

In addition, the state has its share of winning college football teams. The University of Texas, Texas Christian University, Southern Methodist University, and Texas A&M all have won NCAA championships over the years.

Rodeo is an important sport in Texas throughout the year. Professional rodeo evolved in the 1800s from cowboy contests in roping and riding. Now the best-known rodeo events are bull riding, bareback riding, and saddle bronco riding. In these events a rider must stay on top of a bucking bull or horse for at least eight seconds while holding on with just one hand.

Steer wrestling pits a cowboy and a horse against a steer running alongside them. The cowboy must move from the horse to the steer and then wrestle the steer to the ground by turning its horns. Calf roping involves a rider lassoing a running calf with a rope. The cowboy then jumps off the horse and quickly ties up the calf's legs.

The San Antonio Spurs have become a dominant team in the National Basketball Association. The Spurs won NBA Championships in 1999, 2003, 2005, and 2007.

Nolan Ryan, born in Refugio and raised in Alvin, threw a record 5,714 strikeouts and seven no-hitters during his 27-year baseball career. In 2010, he became a co-owner of the Texas Rangers.

The Heisman trophy is named for John William Heisman. He was the first full-time coach and athletic director at Rice University in Houston. The trophy is awarded annually to the top college football player.

Babe Didrikson Zaharias, a Port Arthur native, was one of the best female golfers of all time. She also won two gold medals in track and field at the 1932 Summer Olympics.

The West of the Pecos Rodeo, which takes place every year on July 4, was first held in 1883. It is among the oldest rodeos in the United States.

National Averages Comparison

The United States is a federal republic, consisting of fifty states and the District of Columbia. Alaska and Hawai'i are the only non-contiguous, or non-touching, states in the nation. Today, the United States of America is the third-largest country in the world in population. The United States Census Bureau takes a census, or count of all the people, every ten years. It also regularly collects other kinds of data about the population and the economy. How does Texas compare to the national average?

Comparison Chart

United States 2010 Census Data *	USA	Texas
Admission to Union	NA	December 29, 1845
Land Area (in square miles)	3,537,438.44	261,797.12
Population Total	308,745,538	25,145,561
Population Density (people per square mile)	87.28	96.05
Population Percentage Change (April 1, 2000, to April 1, 2010)	9.7%	20.6%
White Persons (percent)	72.4%	70.4%
Black Persons (percent)	12.6%	11.8%
American Indian and Alaska Native Persons (percent)	0.9%	0.7%
Asian Persons (percent)	4.8%	3.8%
Native Hawaiian and Other Pacific Islander Persons (percent)	0.2%	0.1%
Some Other Race (percent)	6.2%	10.5%
Persons Reporting Two or More Races (percent)	2.9%	2.7%
Persons of Hispanic or Latino Origin (percent)	16.3%	37.6%
Not of Hispanic or Latino Origin (percent)	83.7%	62.4%
Median Household Income	$52,029	$50,049
Percentage of People Age 25 or Over Who Have Graduated from High School	80.4%	75.7%

*All figures are based on the 2010 United States Census, with the exception of the last two items.

How to Improve My Community

Strong communities make strong states. Think about what features are important in your community. What do you value? Education? Health? Forests? Safety? Beautiful spaces? Government works to help citizens create ideal living conditions that are fair to all by providing services in communities. Consider what changes you could make in your community. How would they improve your state as a whole? Using this concept web as a guide, write a report that outlines the features you think are most important in your community and what improvements could be made. A strong state needs strong communities.

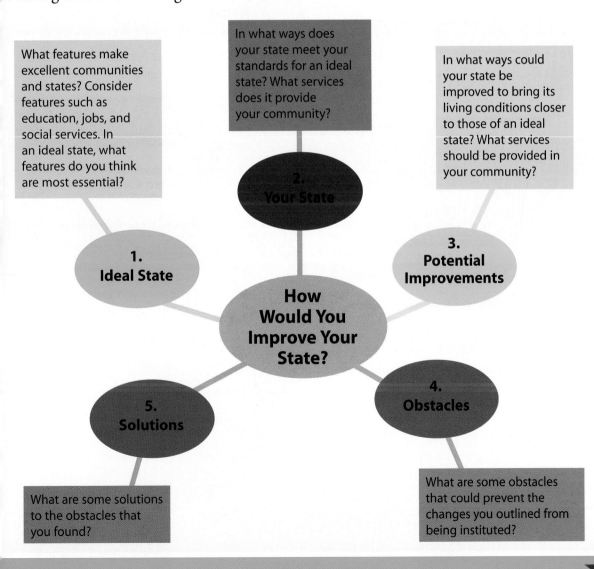

What features make excellent communities and states? Consider features such as education, jobs, and social services. In an ideal state, what features do you think are most essential?

In what ways does your state meet your standards for an ideal state? What services does it provide your community?

In what ways could your state be improved to bring its living conditions closer to those of an ideal state? What services should be provided in your community?

2.
Your State

1.
Ideal State

3.
Potential Improvements

How Would You Improve Your State?

4.
Obstacles

5.
Solutions

What are some solutions to the obstacles that you found?

What are some obstacles that could prevent the changes you outlined from being instituted?

Exercise Your Mind!

Think about these questions and then use your research skills to find the answers and learn more fascinating facts about Texas. A teacher, librarian, or parent may be able to help you locate the best sources to use in your research.

1 Texas is the only state to have had the flags of six different nations fly over it. Which flags are they?

2 How many U.S. presidents were born in Texas?

3 What endangered species makes its winter home in the Aransas National Wildlife Refuge?

4 How many official state pastries does Texas have?

5 The first word spoken on the moon was the name of a Texas city. Which city was it?

6 Why did early settlers in Texas build homes out of grass and dirt?

7 Texas entered the Union in a different way than any other state. How?

8 What Texas animals were called "Hoover hogs"?

Words to Know

allies: people who are friendly with one another or who have made an agreement to work together

ancestry: a person's family background

barren: lacking any useful plant life

commercial: sold for profit

conservation: preservation or protection of natural resources

cuisine: style of preparing food

irrigation: using ditches, streams, or pipes to bring water to dry land

nomads: people with no fixed home who move from one place to another looking for food

ports: harbors where ships dock

precipitation: water that falls from the sky, whether in the form of rain, snow, sleet, hail, or mist

Pulitzer Prize: any of a series of annual prizes awarded for outstanding achievement in American journalism, letters, and music

republic: a country governed by an elected government

resorts: places people go to for relaxation and recreation

rivets: metal bolts or pins

Index

agriculture 24
Alamo 10, 21, 29, 30, 31
allies 27
Austin 7, 8, 9
Austin, Moses 30
Austin, Stephen 30, 32

Big Bend National Park 11, 20
Bush, George W. 33

Caddo Lake 10
cattle 5, 23, 24, 30, 39
Civil War 29
conservation 18
constitution 36
cotton 23, 24, 25, 30
cowboy 5, 39, 43

Dallas 7, 30, 34, 35, 41

El Capitan 10
electronics 23, 25

farms and farmland 16, 23, 24, 30
flags 5, 8

Fort Worth 7, 34

Galveston Island 21
Guadalupe Mountains National Park 10, 20, 21

House of Representatives 36, 37
Houston 7, 30, 32, 34, 35
Houston, Sam 32
hurricane 13

irrigation 23

Johnson, Lyndon B. 20, 33
Jordan, Barbara 33

Kay, Mary 33

Latin America 38
Louisiana 8, 10, 41

McMurtry, Larry 41
Mexico 5, 7, 8, 20, 28, 29, 30, 31, 34, 38, 39

mining 22, 23
missions 20, 28, 29, 30, 31

Nimitz, Chester 33
nomads 26

oil/petroleum 4, 5, 15, 22, 23, 25

Padre Island National Seashore 11
port 15
Porter, Katherine Anne 41

Republic of Texas 4, 5, 9, 29, 31
Rio Grande 7, 8, 10, 11, 13, 24, 26, 28, 29
rodeos 5, 39, 43

San Antonio 7, 20, 30, 35, 40
Senate 36, 37
sheep 24
Space Center Houston 20
Spain 5, 28, 29, 30, 38
state fair 41

tornadoes 13

Log on to www.av2books.com

AV² by Weigl brings you media enhanced books that support active learning. Go to www.av2books.com, and enter the special code found on page 2 of this book. You will gain access to enriched and enhanced content that supplements and complements this book. Content includes video, audio, web links, quizzes, a slide show, and activities.

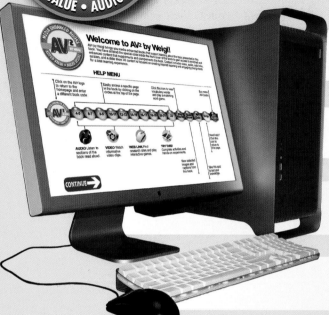

Audio
Listen to sections of the book read aloud.

Video
Watch informative video clips.

Embedded Weblinks
Gain additional information for research.

Try This!
Complete activities and hands-on experiments.

WHAT'S ONLINE?

Try This!	**Embedded Weblinks**	**Video**	**EXTRA FEATURES**
Test your knowledge of the state in a mapping activity.	Discover more attractions in Texas.	Watch a video introduction to Texas.	**Audio** Listen to sections of the book read aloud.
Find out more about precipitation in your city.	Learn more about the history of the state.	Watch a video about the features of the state.	
Plan what attractions you would like to visit in the state.	Learn the full lyrics of the state song.		**Key Words** Study vocabulary, and complete a matching word activity.
Learn more about the early natural resources of the state.			
Write a biography about a notable resident of Texas.			**Slide Show** View images and captio and prepare a presenta
Complete an educational census activity.			**Quizzes** Test your knowledge.

AV² was built to bridge the gap between print and digital. We encourage you to tell us what you like and what you want to see in the future.

Sign up to be an AV² Ambassador at www.av2books.com/ambassador.